American Ball[et Theatre]

MW00591124

Dance photography by Paul B. Goode

Pomegranate
Artbooks
San Francisco

A book of postcards

Pomegranate Artbooks
Box 6099
Rohnert Park, CA 94927

ISBN 1-56640-307-3
Pomegranate Catalog No. A662

Pomegranate publishes books of postcards on a wide range of subjects.
Please write to the publisher for more information

Designed by Allen Boyce Eddington
Printed in Korea

*R*ecognized as a national treasure since its founding in 1940, American Ballet Theatre annually tours the United States and has made a number of international tours. The aim at ABT's inception was to develop a reportoire of the best ballets from the past and to encourage the creation of new works. The reportoire now includes all of the great full-length ballets of the nineteenth century (<u>Swan Lake</u>, <u>The Sleeping Beauty</u>, <u>Othello</u>, etc.), the finest works from the early twentieth century (<u>Apollo</u>, <u>Rodeo</u>, etc.) and acclaimed contemporary masterpieces (<u>Airs</u>, <u>Push Comes to Shove</u>, etc.). In this book of postcards internationally renowned dance photographer Paul B. Goode presents thirty elegant images of ABT at work.

*P*aul B. Goode began to photograph American Ballet Theatre on December 15, 1982, with a portrait session of Mikhail Baryshnikov. In 1985 Goode began a collaboration with ABT's six yearly journals covering the company's rehearsals and performances from that year. These journals included the great classical ballets <u>Romeo and Juliet</u>, <u>The Sleeping Beauty</u> and <u>Swan Lake</u>. The last of the journals illustrated ABT's Fiftieth Anniversary Season in 1990.

On December 18, 1992, Goode began his second decade photographing ABT with a portrait session of its new director, Kevin McKenzie.

Goode's photographs have appeared in <u>American Photo</u>, <u>The New York Times</u>, <u>Essence</u>, <u>Ladies' Home Journal</u>, <u>Dance Magazine</u> and <u>Female Bodybuilding</u>, among others.

*A*t the time of my first experience with American Ballet Theatre, when I was hired to do a portrait of then-director/dancer Mikhail Baryshnikov, I had little knowledge of or interest in classical ballet but hoped to bring the dancers into my studio for formal portraits.

After several portrait sessions with the dancers I was invited to photograph various rehearsals and performances. I took this as a challenge to create something new in ballet photography. I had no interest in capturing on film the dancers' technical ability. My goal was to capture that instant of greatest emotional intensity. I was looking for beauty and romance. I wanted my images to have energy—to appear ready to explode off the paper.

ABT gave me the chance to fulfill this vision by allowing me to shoot from the backstage wings. From this angle the dancers' technique no longer proved to be most important. I was so close to the dancers that I could catch every nuance of their movement, every expression. Shooting backstage, I almost felt part of the performance. Dancers spoke to me before their entrance onstage, brushed past me during their exits. I could feel their energy. I could match their rhythm. I could not help but photograph the dancers at their best.

—*Paul B. Goode*

A m e r i c a n B a l l e t T h e a t r e
Corps warming up for Harald Lander's <u>Études</u>

Pomegranate, Box 6099, Rohnert Park, CA 94927

A m e r i c a n B a l l e t T h e a t r e
Susan Jaffe as Odette in Act IV of <u>Swan Lake</u>

Pomegranate, Box 6099, Rohnert Park, CA 94927

A m e r i c a n   B a l l e t   T h e a t r e
Alessandra Ferri as Juliet in <u>Romeo and Juliet</u>

Pomegranate, Box 6099, Rohnert Park, CA 94927

A m e r i c a n   B a l l e t   T h e a t r e
Julie Kent performing in <u>Les Sylphides</u>

Pomegranate, Box 6099, Rohnert Park, CA 94927

American Ballet Theatre
Danilo Radojevic (sailor) and Christopher Mattox
in Jerome Robbins's <u>Fancy Free</u>

Pomegranate, Box 6099, Rohnert Park, CA 94927

Photograph © Paul B. Goode

A m e r i c a n B a l l e t T h e a t r e
Kathleen Moore in Agnes de Mille's <u>The Informer</u>

Pomegranate, Box 6099, Rohnert Park, CA 94927

American Ballet Theatre
Victor Barbee, Kathleen Moore and John
Gardner (left to right) in Agnes de Mille's <u>Rodeo</u>

Pomegranate, Box 6099, Rohnert Park, CA 94927

Photograph © Paul B. Goode

A m e r i c a n B a l l e t T h e a t r e
Susan Jaffe in George Balanchine's <u>Stravinsky</u>
<u>Violin Concerto</u>

Pomegranate, Box 6099, Rohnert Park, CA 94927

A m e r i c a n B a l l e t T h e a t r e
Kevin McKenzie and Dana Stackpole in Twyla
Tharp's <u>Nine Sinatra Songs</u>

Pomegranate, Box 6099, Rohnert Park, CA 94927

A m e r i c a n   B a l l e t   T h e a t r e
Victor Barbee in Agnes de Mille's <u>The Informer</u>

Pomegranate, Box 6099, Rohnert Park, CA 94927

American Ballet Theatre
Roger Van Fleteren as "The Other" in Agnes de Mille's <u>The Other</u>

Pomegranate, Box 6099, Rohnert Park, CA 94927

Photograph © Paul B. Goode

American Ballet Theatre
Cynthia Harvey putting the finishing touches on her makeup for the role of Juliet in <u>Romeo and Juliet</u>

Pomegranate, Box 6099, Rohnert Park, CA 94927

A m e r i c a n B a l l e t T h e a t r e
Christine Dunham preparing for her entrance
in <u>Les Sylphides</u>

Pomegranate, Box 6099, Rohnert Park, CA 94927

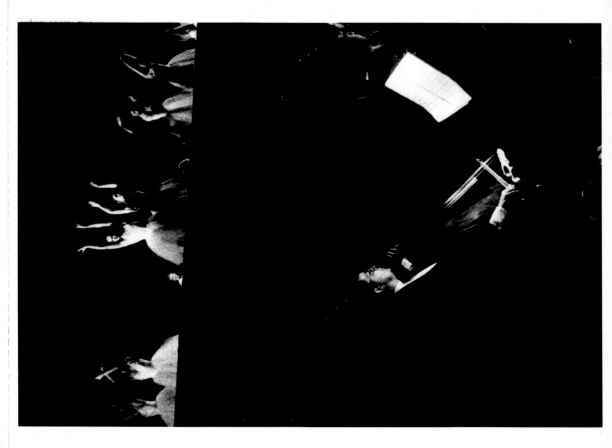

A m e r i c a n B a l l e t T h e a t r e
Musicians and corps performing in Act II of
<u>*Swan Lake*</u>

Pomegranate, Box 6099, Rohnert Park, CA 94927

A m e r i c a n   B a l l e t   T h e a t r e
Antony Tudor rehearsing Michael Owen in his
<u>*Jardin aux Lilas*</u>

Pomegranate, Box 6099, Rohnert Park, CA 94927

A m e r i c a n   B a l l e t   T h e a t r e
*Danilo Radojevic as the Prodigal Son in George
Balanchine's <u>Prodigal Son</u>*

Pomegranate; Box 6099, Rohnert Park, CA 94927

A m e r i c a n B a l l e t T h e a t r e
Susan Jaffe rehearsing for Antony Tudor's
<u>*Jardin aux Lilas*</u>

Pomegranate, Box 6099, Rohnert Park, CA 94927

A m e r i c a n B a l l e t T h e a t r e
Jeremy Collins and Elizabeth Carr in Clark
Tippet's <u>Bruch Violin Concerto No. 1</u>

Pomegranate, Box 6099, Rohnert Park, CA 94927

A merican B allet T heatre
Cheryl Yeager as Princess Aurora and Julio
Bocca as Prince Desire in <u>The Sleeping Beauty</u>

Pomegranate, Box 6099, Rohnert Park, CA 94927

A m e r i c a n   B a l l e t   T h e a t r e
Michael Owen as Carabosse in <u>The Sleeping Beauty</u>

Pomegranate, Box 6099, Rohnert Park, CA 94927

A merica n B allet T h e a t r e
Amanda McKerrow and Kevin McKenzie in
Antony Tudor's The Leaves Are Fading

Pomegranate, Box 6099, Rohnert Park, CA 94927

Photograph © Paul B. Goode

A m e r i c a n   B a l l e t   T h e a t r e
*Marianna Tcherkassky performing the Mad
Scene in the title role of <u>Giselle</u>*

Pomegranate, Box 6099, Rohnert Park, CA 94927

A m e r i c a n   B a l l e t   T h e a t r e
Amanda McKerrow rehearsing the role of
Princess Aurora for <u>The Sleeping Beauty</u>

Pomegranate, Box 6099, Rohnert Park, CA 94927

A m e r i c a n B a l l e t T h e a t r e
Ross Stretton and Cynthia Harvey in Sir Kenneth
MacMillan's <u>Requiem</u>

Pomegranate, Box 6099, Rohnert Park, CA 94927

Photograph © Paul B. Goode

American Ballet Theatre
Julie Kent rehearsing for George Balanchine's
<u>*Stravinsky Violin Concerto*</u>

Pomegranate, Box 6099, Rohnert Park, CA 94927

A m e r i c a n   B a l l e t   T h e a t r e
The corps in the opening moment of Act IV,
<u>*Swan Lake*</u>

Pomegranate, Box 6099, Rohnert Park, CA 94927

American Ballet Theatre
Jeremy Collins in the role of the Dance Master in
Leonide Massine's <u>*Gaîté Parisienne*</u>

Pomegranate, Box 6099, Rohnert Park, CA 94927

Photograph © Paul B. Goode

A m e r i c a n B a l l e t T h e a t r e
Leslie Browne performing in Antony Tudor's
<u>*Jardin aux Lilas*</u>

Pomegranate, Box 6099, Rohnert Park, CA 94927

A m e r i c a n B a l l e t T h e a t r e
Susan Jaffe as Princess Aurora in <u>The Sleeping</u>
<u>*Beauty*</u>

Pomegranate. Box 6099, Rohnert Park, CA 94927

Photograph © Paul B. Goode